loaves, cakes &
Quiches
with friends

Recipes by Ilona
Photographs by Akiko Ida

HACHETTE
Illustrated

contents

tips & advice

Pesto

Pesto, sometimes called *pistou*, is a thick sauce made from basil, pine nuts, garlic and olive oil. It is available ready-made in jars, or in the fresh sauce section of large supermarkets. It can also be found at some Italian delicatessens.

To make 150 g (5 oz) pesto:
- 3 bunches of fresh basil
- 3 garlic cloves
- 50 g (1¾ oz) pine nuts
- 4 tablespoons Parmesan cheese, freshly grated
- 100 ml (3½ fl oz) olive oil
- pinch of coarse salt

Parmesan shortcrust pastry

- 250 g (8 oz) plain flour
- pinch of salt
- 30 g (1 oz) Parmesan cheese, grated
- 125 g (4 oz) unsalted butter, diced
- 1 egg
- 1 teaspoon crème fraîche

Put the flour and salt into a large bowl. Add the butter and with a knife cut it into the flour until evenly distributed, then use your fingertips to rub the fat lightly into the flour until the mixture resembles coarse crumbs. Stir in the cheese. Whisk together the egg and crème fraîche and gradually add to the crumb mixture (you may not need all of it). Using a spatula or a knife, work the mixture together, then use your fingers until you have a smooth dough. Shape into a ball, place in a polythene bag and refrigerate for 1 hour before using.

Sun-dried tomatoes

An authentic Italian *antipasto* ingredient, these are actually made by drying in the sun.
To make your own, cut some tomatoes in half, sprinkle with salt and leave to drain. Arrange the halves on a grill rack set over a baking tin to catch the drips. Put in the oven and bake gently at 150°C (300°F) gas mark 2, for about 3 hours.
Allow to cool completely, then marinate in a lidded glass jar with garlic, olive oil, salt and pepper.
Sun-dried tomatoes can also be bought loose, in packets or in jars from supermarkets and delicatessens.

Poppyseeds

These can be found in the herbs and spices sections of large supermarkets, as well as in health food shops and delicatessens.

Sweet hazelnut and chocolate pastry

- 250 g (8 oz) plain flour
- pinch of salt
- 70 g (2½ oz) caster sugar
- 50 g (1¾ oz) ground hazelnuts
- 2 tablespoons unsweetened cocoa powder
- 125 g (4 oz) unsalted butter
- 1 egg
- 1 teaspoon crème fraîche

Put the flour and salt into a large bowl. Stir in the sugar, ground hazelnuts and cocoa. Add the butter and with a knife cut it into the flour mixture until evenly distributed, then using your fingertips rub the fat lightly into the flour until the mixture resembles coarse crumbs. Whisk together the egg and crème fraîche and add gradually to the mixture (you may not need all of it). Work together using a spatula or a knife, then use your fingers to form a smooth ball of dough. Place in a polythene bag and refrigerate for 1 hour before using.

Bicarbonate of soda

This fine white powder is an indispensable ingredient when baking sweet cakes. It lightens the mixture and makes it easier to digest. It is readily available in supermarkets and sometimes at the chemist's (be sure to indicate that it is for culinary use). Always use the quantities indicated in the recipe.

Tomato, basil and mozzarella quiche

For the shortcrust pastry
250 g (8 oz) plain flour
pinch of salt
125 g (4 oz) unsalted butter,
diced
1 egg
1 teaspoon crème fraîche

For the filling
500 g (1 lb) tomatoes
125 g (4 oz) mozzarella
large handful of fresh basil
3 eggs
200 ml (7 fl oz) crème fraîche
salt and pepper

To make the pastry for 1 large tart or 5 small tarts: put the flour and salt into a large bowl. Add the butter and with a knife cut it into the flour until evenly distributed, then use your fingertips to rub the fat lightly into the flour until the mixture resembles coarse crumbs. Whisk together the egg and crème fraîche and add gradually to the crumb mixture (you may not need to use all of it). Using a spatula or a knife, work the mixture together, then use your fingers until you have a smooth dough. Shape into a ball, place in a polythene bag and refrigerate for 1 hour before using.

Meanwhile, prepare the filling. Place the tomatoes in a bowl and pour over boiling water to cover. Leave for 1–2 minutes, then drain, cut a cross at the stem end of each tomato, and peel off the skins. Deseed and chop the flesh. Cut the mozzarella into small cubes. Tear the basil leaves in small pieces by hand or snip with scissors. Whisk together the eggs and crème fraîche and season with salt and pepper.

Preheat the oven to 190°C (375°F) gas mark 5. Lightly butter a loose-based flan tin. Roll out the dough and use to line the tin. Prick the base with a fork.

Arrange the chopped tomato in the pastry shell and add the cheese cubes. Sprinkle with the basil leaves and pour over the egg mixture. Bake for 40 minutes. Allow to cool before turning out.

Pumpkin and cheese quiche

For the shortcrust pastry
250 g (8 oz) plain flour
pinch of salt
125 g (4 oz) unsalted butter,
diced
1 egg
1 teaspoon crème fraîche

For the filling
500 g (1 lb) pumpkin
20 g (³/₄ oz) unsalted butter
3 eggs
100 g (3¹/₂ oz) grated
cheese, such as Gruyère
200 ml (7 fl oz) crème fraîche
handful of fresh coriander,
finely chopped
salt and pepper

To make the pastry: put the flour and salt into a large bowl. Add the butter and with a knife cut it into the flour until evenly distributed, then use your fingertips to rub the fat lightly into the flour until the mixture resembles coarse crumbs. Whisk together the egg and crème fraîche and add gradually to the crumb mixture (you may not need to use all of it). Using a spatula or a knife, work the mixture together, then use your fingers until you have a smooth dough. Shape into a ball, put into a polythene bag and refrigerate for 1 hour before using.

Preheat the oven to 190°C (375°F) gas mark 5. Lightly butter a loose-based flan tin and line with the rolled-out pastry. Prick the base with a fork. Refrigerate until needed.

To make the filling: peel and deseed the pumpkin, then cut into small cubes. Melt the butter in a pan, add the pumpkin and cook until tender, about 10 minutes. Add a little water and continue cooking until the pumpkin is tender. Purée and allow to cool.

In a bowl, whisk together the eggs, cheese and crème fraîche. Add the pumpkin purée and mix well. Stir in the chopped coriander and season to taste with salt and pepper.

Pour the filling into the pastry shell and bake for 40 minutes until set. Allow to cool slightly before serving.

Spicy onion quiche

For the shortcrust pastry
250 g (8 oz) plain flour
pinch of salt
125 g (4 oz) unsalted butter,
diced
1 egg
1 teaspoon crème fraîche

For the filling
50 g (1³/₄ oz) unsalted butter
1 kg (2 lb) onions, chopped
100 ml (3¹/₂ floz) dry white wine
1 red chilli, deseeded and
finely chopped
3 eggs
200 ml (7 fl oz) crème fraîche
125 g (4oz) finely grated
cheese, such as Gruyère
salt and pepper

To make the pastry: put the flour and salt into a large bowl. Add the butter and with a knife cut it into the flour until evenly distributed, then use your fingertips to rub the fat lightly into the flour until the mixture resembles coarse crumbs. Whisk together the egg and crème fraîche and add gradually to the crumb mixture (you may not need to use all of it). Using a spatula or a knife, work the mixture together, then use your fingers until you have a smooth dough. Shape into a ball, put into a polythene bag and refrigerate for 1 hour before using.

Preheat the oven to 190°C (375°F) gas mark 5. Lightly butter a loose-based flan tin and line with the rolled-out pastry. Prick the base with a fork and refrigerate until needed.

To make the filling: melt the butter in a pan, add the onions and cook until soft. Add the wine and chilli and simmer gently for 20 minutes. Set aside to cool.

Whisk the eggs in a large bowl. Add the crème fraîche and the onions and mix well. Season with salt and pepper.

Pour the onion mixture into the pastry shell, sprinkle with the cheese and bake for about 45 minutes. Allow to cool slightly before serving.

Mustard and cheese quiche

For the shortcrust pastry
250 g (8 oz) plain flour
pinch of salt
125 g (4 oz) unsalted butter,
diced
1 egg
1 teaspoon crème fraîche

For the filling
3 eggs
100 ml (3$\frac{1}{2}$ fl oz) milk
200 ml (7 fl oz) crème fraîche
150 g (5oz) wholegrain mustard
100 g (3$\frac{1}{2}$ oz) grated cheese,
such as Gruyère
salt and pepper

To make the pastry: put the flour and salt into a large bowl. Add the butter and with a knife cut it into the flour until evenly distributed, then use your fingertips to rub the fat lightly into the flour until the mixture resembles coarse crumbs. Whisk together the egg and crème fraîche and add gradually to the crumb mixture (you may not need to use all of it). Using a spatula or a knife, work the mixture together, then use your fingers until you have a smooth dough. Shape into a ball, put into a polythene bag and refrigerate for 1 hour before using.

Preheat the oven to 190°C (375°F) gas mark 5. Lightly butter a loose-based flan tin. Roll out the dough and use to line the tin. Prick the base with a fork. Refrigerate until needed.

To make the filling: in a bowl, whisk together the eggs, milk and crème fraîche. Add the mustard and cheese and mix well. Season with salt and pepper.

Pour the mustard mixture into the pastry shell and bake for about 40 minutes. Allow to cool slightly before serving.

Spinach and ricotta quiche

For the shortcrust pastry
250 g (8 oz) plain flour
pinch of salt
125 g (4 oz) unsalted butter,
diced
1 egg
1 teaspoon crème fraîche

For the filling
500 g (1 lb) fresh spinach
20 g ($^3/_4$ oz) unsalted butter
3 eggs
200 g (7 oz) ricotta
100 ml (3$^1/_2$ fl oz) crème
fraîche
pinch of freshly grated
nutmeg
salt and pepper

To make the pastry: put the flour and salt into a large bowl. Add the butter and with a knife cut it into the flour until evenly distributed, then use your fingertips to rub the fat lightly into the flour until the mixture resembles coarse crumbs. Whisk together the egg and crème fraîche and add gradually to the crumb mixture (you may not need to use all of it). Using a spatula or a knife, work the mixture together, then use your fingers until you have a smooth dough. Shape into a ball, put into a polythene bag and refrigerate for 1 hour before using.

Preheat the oven to 190°C (375°F) gas mark 5. Lightly butter a loose-based flan tin and line with the rolled-out pastry. Prick the base with a fork. Refrigerate until needed.

To make the filling: Wash the spinach, remove stems and pat dry. Heat the butter in a large saucepan. Add the spinach and cook for about 8 minutes. Transfer to a colander, drain thoroughly and squeeze out as much water as possible, then chop coarsely.

In a large bowl, whisk together the eggs, ricotta and crème fraîche. Stir in the spinach. Season with nutmeg, salt and pepper.

Pour into the pastry shell and bake for about 40 minutes until firm and golden. Allow to cool slightly before serving.

Munster cheese and bacon quiche

For the shortcrust pastry
250 g (8 oz) plain flour
pinch of salt
125 g (4 oz) unsalted butter,
diced
1 egg
1 teaspoon crème fraîche

For the filling
30 g (1oz) unsalted butter
200 g (7 oz) smoked bacon,
coarsely chopped
3 onions, chopped
2 garlic cloves, crushed
3 tablespoons beer
200 ml (7 fl oz) crème fraîche
250 g (8 oz) Munster cheese,
thinly sliced
small pinch of cumin seeds
salt and pepper

To make the pastry: put the flour and salt into a large bowl. Add the butter and with a knife cut it into the flour until evenly distributed, then use your fingertips to rub the fat lightly into the flour until the mixture resembles coarse crumbs. Whisk together the egg and crème fraîche and add gradually to the crumb mixture (you may not need to use all of it). Using a spatula or a knife, work the mixture together, then use your fingers until you have a smooth dough. Shape into a ball, put into a polythene bag and refrigerate for 1 hour before using.

Preheat the oven to 190°C (375°F) gas mark 5. Lightly butter a loose-based flan tin and line with the rolled-out pastry. Prick the base with a fork and refrigerate until needed.

To make the filling: melt the butter in a frying pan. Add the bacon and cook until browned. Add the onions and cook until golden. Add the garlic, beer, crème fraîche and half of the cheese. Simmer gently for 3 minutes. Season with cumin seeds, salt and pepper.

Pour into the pastry shell and top with the remaining slices of cheese. Bake for 20 minutes until golden.

Tuna and vegetable quiche

For the shortcrust pastry
250 g (8 oz) plain flour
pinch of salt
125 g (4 oz) unsalted butter,
diced
1 egg
1 teaspoon crème fraîche

For the filling
oil
1 onion, chopped
2 garlic cloves, crushed
1x400 g (14 oz) can peeled whole
tomatoes, drained
pinch of dried thyme
4 eggs
250–275 g (8–9 oz) can tuna in brine
150 g (5 oz) peas, fresh or frozen
125 g (4 oz) grated cheese,
such as Gruyère
salt and pepper

To make the pastry: put the flour and salt into a large bowl. Add the butter and with a knife cut it into the flour until evenly distributed, then use your fingertips to rub the fat lightly into the flour until the mixture resembles coarse crumbs. Whisk together the egg and crème fraîche and add gradually to the crumb mixture (you may not need to use all of it). Using a spatula or a knife, work the mixture together, then use your fingers until you have a smooth dough. Shape into a ball, put into a polythene bag and refrigerate for 1 hour before using.

Preheat the oven to 190°C (375°F) gas mark 5. Lightly butter a loose-based flan tin and line with the rolled-out pastry. Prick the base with a fork and refrigerate until needed.

To make the filling: heat some oil in a pan and fry the onion and garlic until soft. Add the tomatoes and simmer gently for 20 minutes. Sprinkle with thyme and allow to cool.

Drain and flake the tuna. Whisk the eggs in a large bowl. Stir in the tuna, peas and tomato mixture. Season with salt and pepper. Pour into the pastry shell, sprinkle with the cheese and bake for about 45 minutes. Allow to cool slightly before serving.

Feta cheese and fresh herb loaf

180 g (6½ oz) plain flour
3 teaspoons baking powder
3 eggs
100 g (3½ fl oz) olive oil
1 tablespoon sunflower oil
100 ml (3½ fl oz) milk
200 g (7 oz) feta cheese, cubed
100 g (3½ oz) grated cheese,
such as Gruyère
2–3 handfuls of mixed fresh herbs
(basil, parsley, chives), chopped
salt and pepper

Preheat the oven to 180°C (350°F) gas mark 4. Grease a loaf tin and lightly dust with flour.

In a large bowl, mix together the flour and baking powder. In another bowl, whisk together the eggs, both oils and the milk. Season with salt and pepper.

Pour the egg mixture into the flour mixture and fold in gently to combine. Stir in the feta, grated cheese and fresh herbs.

Pour the mixture into the prepared tin and bake for about 50 minutes, until the tip of a knife inserted in the centre of the loaf comes out clean. Allow to cool in the tin before turning out.

Parma ham and fig loaf

180 g (6½ oz) plain flour
3 teaspoons baking powder
3 eggs
100 g (3½ fl oz) olive oil
100 ml (3½ fl oz) milk
100 g (3½ oz) grated cheese,
such as Gruyère
200 g (7 oz) fresh figs
100 g (3½ oz) Parma ham, cut in strips
salt and pepper

Preheat the oven to 180°C (350°F) gas mark 4. Grease a loaf tin and lightly dust with flour.

In a large bowl, mix together the flour and baking powder. In another bowl, whisk together the eggs, oil and the milk. Season with salt and pepper.

Pour the egg mixture into the flour mixture and fold in gently until there are no more lumps. Stir in the grated cheese, figs (whole or chopped) and ham and mix gently.

Pour the mixture into the prepared tin and bake for about 50 minutes, until the tip of a knife inserted in the centre of the loaf comes out clean. Allow to cool in the tin before turning out.

Roquefort, pear and walnut loaf

180 g (6½ oz) plain flour
3 teaspoons baking powder
3 eggs
4 teaspoons walnut oil
100 ml (3½ fl oz) sunflower oil
100 ml (3½ fl oz) milk
100 g (3½ oz) grated cheese,
such as Gruyère
150 g (5 oz) Roquefort cheese,
crumbled
2 pears, peeled and cubed
100 g (3½ oz) walnut pieces
salt and pepper

Preheat the oven to 180°C (350°F) gas mark 4. Grease a loaf tin and lightly dust with flour.

In a large bowl, mix the flour and baking powder. In another bowl, whisk together the eggs, both the oils and the milk. Season with salt and pepper.

Pour the egg mixture into the flour mixture and fold in gently. Add the grated cheese and mix well. Stir in the Roquefort, pears and walnut pieces until blended.

Pour the mixture into the prepared tin and bake for about 50 minutes, until the tip of a knife inserted in the centre of the loaf comes out clean. Allow to cool in the tin before turning out.

Mushroom loaf

unsalted butter
300 g (11 oz) mixed mushrooms, sliced
2 shallots, chopped
180 g (6½ oz) plain flour
3 teaspoons baking powder
3 eggs
125 ml (4 fl oz) sunflower oil
100 ml 3½ fl oz) milk
100 g (3½ oz) grated cheese,
such as Gruyère
1 handful of fresh parsley, chopped
salt and pepper

Preheat the oven to 180°C (350°F) gas mark 4. Grease a loaf tin and lightly dust with flour.

Heat a knob of butter in a pan, add the mushrooms and cook until all the liquid has evaporated. Add the shallots and cook for 1 minute more. Set aside to cool.

In a large bowl, mix the flour and baking powder. In another bowl, whisk together the eggs, oil and the milk. Season with salt and pepper.

Pour the egg mixture into the flour mixture and fold in gently. Stir in the grated cheese and parsley. Add the mushroom mixture and mix to blend.

Pour the mixture into the prepared tin and bake for about 50 minutes, until the tip of a knife inserted in the centre of the loaf comes out clean. Allow to cool in the tin before turning out.

Courgette and Parmesan loaf

250 g (8 oz) courgettes
20 g ($^3/_4$ oz) unsalted butter
200 g (7 oz) plain flour
3 teaspoons baking powder
3 eggs
50 ml (1$^3/_4$ fl oz) sunflower oil
50 ml (1$^3/_4$ fl oz) olive oil
100 ml (3$^1/_2$ fl oz) milk
100 g (3$^1/_2$ oz) grated cheese,
such as Gruyère
100 g (3$^1/_2$ oz) grated Parmesan
cheese
handful of fresh basil, chopped
handful of fresh mint, chopped
salt and pepper

Wash and dry the courgettes, then grate. Heat the butter in a pan. Stir in the grated courgettes and cook until the liquid has evaporated.

Preheat the oven to 180°C (350°F) gas mark 4. Grease a loaf tin and lightly dust with flour.

In a large bowl, mix the flour and baking powder. In another bowl, whisk together the eggs, both oils and the milk. Season with salt and pepper.

Pour the egg mixture into the flour mixture and fold in gently. Stir in the grated cheese, Parmesan, basil, mint and courgettes. Mix well.

Pour the mixture into the prepared tin and bake for about 50 minutes, until the tip of a knife inserted in the centre of the loaf comes out clean. Allow to cool in the tin before turning out.

Green and black olive loaf

180 g (6$\frac{1}{2}$ oz) plain flour
3 teaspoons baking powder
3 eggs
100 g (3$\frac{1}{2}$ fl oz) olive oil
100 ml (3$\frac{1}{2}$ fl oz) milk
100 g (3$\frac{1}{2}$ oz) grated cheese,
such as Gruyère
100 g (3$\frac{1}{2}$ oz) smoked bacon,
cut into strips
100 g (3$\frac{1}{2}$ oz) green olives, stoned
100 g (3$\frac{1}{2}$ oz) black olives, stoned
salt and pepper

Preheat the oven to 180°C (350°F) gas mark 4. Grease a loaf tin and lightly dust with flour.

In a large bowl, mix the flour and baking powder. In another bowl, whisk together the eggs, oil and the milk. Season with salt and pepper.

Pour the egg mixture into the flour mixture and fold in gently. Stir in the grated cheese, bacon and all the olives.

Pour the mixture into the prepared tin and bake for about 50 minutes, until the tip of a knife inserted in the centre of the loaf comes out clean. Allow to cool in the tin before turning out.

Bacon, sausage and cheese loaf

150 g (5 oz) plain flour
3 teaspoons baking powder
3 eggs
100 g (3$\frac{1}{2}$ fl oz) walnut oil
100 ml (3$\frac{1}{2}$ fl oz) milk
100 g (3$\frac{1}{2}$ oz) grated cheese,
such as Gruyère
150 g (5 oz) smoked bacon,
cut into strips
100 g (3$\frac{1}{2}$ oz) French-style saucisson
(or salami), chopped
salt and pepper

Preheat the oven to 180°C (350°F) gas mark 4. Grease a loaf tin and lightly dust with flour.

In a large bowl, mix the flour and baking powder. In another bowl, whisk together the eggs, oil and the milk. Season with salt and pepper.

Pour the egg mixture into the flour mixture and fold in gently until there are no more lumps. Stir in the grated cheese, bacon and saucisson. Mix well.

Pour the mixture into the prepared tin and bake for about 50 minutes, until the tip of a knife inserted in the centre of the loaf comes out clean. Allow to cool in the tin before turning out.

Salmon, dill and pink peppercorn loaf

20 g (³/₄ oz) unsalted butter
250 g (8 oz) salmon, smoked or fresh
200 g (7 oz) plain flour
3 teaspoons baking powder
3 eggs
100 ml (3¹/₂ fl oz) sunflower oil
100 ml (3¹/₂ fl oz) milk
100 g (3¹/₂ oz) grated cheese,
such as Gruyère
handful of fresh dill, chopped
2 pinches pink peppercorns, crushed
salt and pepper

Melt the butter in a pan. Cut the salmon into pieces and cook gently in the butter for around 5 minutes.

Preheat the oven to 180°C (350°F) gas mark 4. Grease a loaf tin and lightly dust with flour.

In a large bowl, mix the flour and baking powder. In another bowl, whisk together the eggs, oil and the milk. Season with salt and pepper.

Pour the egg mixture into the flour mixture and fold in gently until there are no more lumps. Stir in the grated cheese, salmon, dill and pink peppercorns. Mix well.

Pour the mixture into the prepared tin and bake for about 50 minutes, until the tip of a knife inserted in the centre of the loaf comes out clean. Allow to cool in the tin before turning out.

Sun-dried tomato, caper and basil loaf

200 g (7 oz) plain flour
3 teaspoons baking powder
3 eggs
100 ml (3½ fl oz) olive oil
100 ml (3½ fl oz) milk
100 g (3½ oz) grated cheese,
such as Gruyère
200 g (7 oz) sun-dried tomatoes,
chopped
50 g (1¾ oz) capers in salt, rinsed
large handful of fresh basil, torn into
small pieces, or snipped with scissors
salt and pepper

Preheat the oven to 180°C (350°F) gas mark 4. Grease a loaf tin and lightly dust with flour.

In a large bowl, mix the flour and baking powder. In another bowl, whisk together the eggs, oil and the milk. Season with salt and pepper.

Pour the egg mixture into the flour mixture and fold in gently until there are no more lumps. Stir in the grated cheese, sun-dried tomatoes, capers and basil. Mix well.

Pour the mixture into the prepared tin and bake for about 45 minutes, until the tip of a knife inserted in the centre of the loaf comes out clean. Allow to cool in the tin before turning out.

Pesto and pine nut loaf

180 g (6½ oz) plain flour
3 teaspoons baking powder
3 eggs
3 tablespoons olive oil
100 ml (3½ fl oz) milk
100 g (3½ oz) grated cheese,
such as Gruyère
150 g (5 oz) pesto
(see below)
large handful of pine nuts
salt and pepper

For the pesto
3 large bunches of basil
3 garlic cloves
50 g (1¾ oz) pine nuts
4 tablespoons Parmesan
cheese, grated
100 ml (3½ fl oz) olive oil
coarse salt

To prepare the pesto: combine the basil leaves, garlic, pine nuts and a pinch of coarse salt in a food processor and blend until smooth. Transfer to a bowl and carefully stir in the Parmesan and oil with a fork.

Preheat the oven to 180°C (350°F) gas mark 4. Grease a loaf tin and lightly dust with flour.

In a large bowl, mix the flour and baking powder. In another bowl, whisk together the eggs, oil and the milk. Season with salt and pepper.

Pour the egg mixture into the flour mixture and fold in gently until there are no more lumps. Stir in the grated cheese, pesto and whole pine nuts. Mix well.

Pour the mixture into the prepared tin and bake for about 50 minutes, until the tip of a knife inserted in the centre of the loaf comes out clean. Allow to cool in the tin before turning out.

Strawberry and rhubarb tart

For the sweet pastry
250 g (8 oz) plain flour
70 g (2½ oz) caster sugar
pinch of salt
125 g (4 oz) unsalted butter
1 egg
1 teaspoon crème fraîche

For the filling
500 g (1 lb) rhubarb
20 g (¾ oz) unsalted butter
150 g (5 oz) caster sugar
200 g (7 oz) strawberries,
trimmed and halved
200 ml (7 fl oz) crème fraîche

To make the pastry: put the flour, sugar and salt into a large bowl. Add the butter and with a knife cut it into the flour until evenly distributed, then use your fingertips to rub the fat lightly into the flour until the mixture resembles coarse crumbs. Whisk together the egg and crème fraîche and add gradually to the crumb mixture (you may not need all of it). Using a spatula or a knife, work the mixture together, then use your fingers until you have a smooth dough. Shape into a ball, put into a polythene bag and refrigerate for 1 hour before using.

Preheat the oven to 190°C (375°F) gas mark 5. Lightly butter a loose-based flan tin. Roll out the dough and use to line the tin. Prick the base with a fork. To bake blind: cover the pastry with a circle of baking parchment weighted down with dry beans or pie weights. Bake for 20 minutes. Take out of the oven and remove weights. Set aside.

To make the filling: trim the rhubarb and cut into pieces. In a saucepan, combine the butter, sugar and rhubarb pieces over low heat and cook until tender. Remove from the heat and stir in the strawberries and crème fraîche.

Spread the rhubarb mixture into the pre-baked tart shell and bake for 20 minutes.

Dark chocolate tart

For the sweet pastry
250 g (8 oz) plain flour
70 g (2$\frac{1}{2}$ oz) caster sugar
pinch of salt
125 g (4 oz) unsalted butter
1 egg
1 teaspoon crème fraîche

For the filling
300 g (11 oz) dark chocolate
(minimum 70% solids)
300 ml (11 oz) whipping cream
80 g (2$\frac{3}{4}$ oz) unsalted butter,
cut into pieces
3 whole eggs plus 3 egg yolks
40 g (1$\frac{1}{2}$ oz) caster sugar

To make the pastry: put the flour, sugar and salt into a large bowl. Add the butter and with a knife cut it into the flour until evenly distributed, then use your fingertips to rub the fat lightly into the flour until the mixture resembles coarse crumbs. Whisk together the egg and crème fraîche and add gradually to the crumb mixture (you may not need all of it). Using a spatula or a knife, work the mixture together, then use your fingers until you have a smooth dough. Shape into a ball, put into a polythene bag and refrigerate for 1 hour before using.

Preheat the oven to 190°C (375°F) gas mark 5. Lightly butter a loose-based flan tin. Roll out the dough and use to line the tin. Prick the base with a fork. To bake blind: cover the pastry with a circle of baking parchment weighted down with dry beans or pie weights. Bake for 20 minutes. Take out of the oven and remove weights. Set aside.

To make the filling: chop the chocolate into very small pieces. Bring the cream to the boil in a saucepan. Remove from the heat and stir in the chocolate and butter until completely melted. In another bowl, whisk together the eggs, egg yolks and sugar. When the chocolate mixture has cooled, stir in the egg mixture.

Lower the oven to 150°C (300°F) gas mark 2. Pour the chocolate mixture into the pre-baked tart shell and bake for 20 minutes. Allow to cool before serving.

Tarte Tatin

For the pastry
250 g (8 oz) plain flour
pinch of salt
125 g (4 oz) unsalted butter
1 egg
1 teaspoon crème fraîche

For the filling
750 g (1³⁄₄ lb) apples
60 g (2¹⁄₄ oz) unsalted butter
100 g (3 oz) caster sugar
pinch of ground cinnamon

To make the pastry: put the flour and salt into a large bowl. Add the butter and with a knife cut it into the flour until evenly distributed, then use your fingertips to rub the fat lightly into the flour until the mixture resembles coarse crumbs. Whisk together the egg and crème fraîche and add gradually to the crumb mixture (you may not need all of it). Using a spatula or a knife, work the mixture together, then use your fingers until you have a smooth dough. Shape into a ball, put into a polythene bag and refrigerate for 1 hour before using.

Preheat the oven to 200°C (400°F) gas mark 6.

To make the filling: peel, core and quarter the apples. Melt the butter in a flameproof pie dish over low heat. Sprinkle a thin layer of sugar over the bottom and add the cinnamon. Stir until the sugar melts and begins to caramelize. Remove from the heat.

Arrange the apple quarters in the dish, working from the outside edge into the centre, until filled. Sprinkle with the remaining sugar and bake for 5–10 minutes.

Roll out the dough and place on top of the apples. Push down gently, then prick all over with a fork. Bake for 25–30 minutes. Remove from the oven and allow to rest for 2 minutes. Turn out onto a plate, so the apples are on the top. Serve warm, with some crème fraîche.

Raspberry conserve tart

For the shortcrust pastry
375 g (13 oz) plain flour
100 g (3½ oz) caster sugar
pinch of salt
200 g (7 oz) unsalted butter
2 eggs
1 tablespoon crème fraîche

For the filling
350 g (12 oz) raspberry
conserve (any red fruit
conserve will work well:
cherry, strawberry, redcurrant)

To make the pastry: put the flour, sugar and salt into a large bowl. Add the butter and with a knife cut it into the flour until evenly distributed, then use your fingertips to rub the fat lightly into the flour until the mixture resembles coarse crumbs. Whisk together the egg and crème fraîche and add gradually to the crumb mixture (you may not need all of it). Using a spatula or a knife, work the mixture together, then use your fingers until you have a smooth dough. Shape into a ball, put into a polythene bag and refrigerate for 1 hour before using.

Preheat the oven to 180°C (350°F) gas mark 4. Lightly butter a loose-based flan tin. Roll out the dough and use to line the tin. Roll out the leftover dough and cut into thin strips. Prick the dough in the tin all over with a fork.

Spread the raspberry conserve in the pastry shell and lay the strips of pastry on top, in a trellis pattern.

Bake for 40 minutes. Allow to cool before serving.

Lemon tart

For the sweet pastry
250 g (8 oz) plain flour
70 g (2½ oz) caster sugar
pinch of salt
125 g (4 oz) unsalted butter
1 egg
1 teaspoon crème fraîche

For the filling
150 ml (5½ fl oz) crème
fraîche
4 eggs
150 g (5 oz) icing sugar
240 ml (8 fl oz) lemon juice
grated zest of 1 lemon

To make the pastry: put the flour, sugar and salt into a large bowl. Add the butter and with a knife cut it into the flour until evenly distributed, then use your fingertips to rub the fat lightly into the flour until the mixture resembles coarse crumbs. Whisk together the egg and crème fraîche and add gradually to the crumb mixture (you may not need all of it). Using a spatula or a knife, work the mixture together, then use your fingers until you have a smooth dough. Shape into a ball, put into a polythene bag and refrigerate for 1 hour before using

Preheat the oven to 190°C (375°F) gas mark 5. Lightly butter a loose-based flan tin, or small individual tins. Roll out the dough and use to line the tin. Prick the base with a fork. To bake blind: cover the pastry with a circle of baking parchment weighted down with dry beans or pie weights. Bake for 10 minutes. Take out of the oven and remove weights. Set aside.

Lower the oven to 140°C (275°F) gas mark 1.

To make the filling: warm the crème fraîche in a saucepan over low heat. In a bowl, whisk together the eggs, sugar and lemon juice. Stir in the warm crème fraîche and the grated lemon zest. Pour the filling into the pre-baked tart shell.

Bake until the filling is just set, about 35 minutes. Allow to cool before turning out. Refrigerate for several hours before serving.

Chestnut tart

For the sweet pastry
250 g (8 oz) plain flour
70 g (2½ oz) caster sugar
pinch of salt
125 g (4 oz) unsalted butter
1 egg
1 teaspoon crème fraîche

For the filling
2 eggs
150 ml (5½ fl oz) crème fraîche
200 g (7 oz) unsweetened
chestnut purée (see note)
125 g (4 oz) honey
50 g (1¾ oz) flaked almonds,
plus a few for decoration

To make the pastry: put the flour, sugar and salt into a large bowl. Add the butter and with a knife cut it into the flour until evenly distributed, then use your fingertips to rub the fat lightly into the flour until the mixture resembles coarse crumbs. Whisk together the egg and crème fraîche and add gradually to the crumb mixture (you may not need all of it). Using a spatula or a knife, work the mixture together, then use your fingers until you have a smooth dough. Shape into a ball, put into a polythene bag and refrigerate for 1 hour before using

Preheat the oven to 190°C (375°F) gas mark 5. Lightly butter a loose-based flan tin. Roll out the dough and use to line the tin. Prick the base with a fork. To bake blind: cover the pastry with a circle of baking parchment weighted down with dry beans or pie weights. Bake for 20 minutes. Take out of the oven and remove weights. Set aside

To make the filling: put the eggs, crème fraîche, chestnut purée, honey and the almonds in a bowl and stir well to blend. Pour into the pre-baked tart shell.

Bake for 20 minutes. Sprinkle with the remaining flaked almonds and allow to cool before serving.

Note: If unsweetened chestnut purée is not available, use canned whole peeled chestnuts and purée in a food processor.

Carrot and walnut cake

2 eggs
125 g (4 oz) caster sugar
200 g (7 oz) plain flour
125 g (4 oz) unsalted butter, melted
2$\frac{1}{2}$ teaspoons baking powder
pinch of bicarbonate of soda
250 g (8 oz) carrots, grated
60 g (2 oz) walnuts, chopped
$\frac{1}{2}$ teaspoon ground cinnamon

Preheat the oven to 180°C (350°F) gas mark 4. Grease a loaf tin and lightly dust with flour.

In a bowl, whisk together the eggs and sugar until thick and frothy. Gradually incorporate the flour and melted butter. With a spatula, fold in the baking powder, bicarbonate of soda, carrots, walnuts and cinnamon. Fold just until well blended.

Pour the mixture into the prepared tin and bake for about 50 minutes, until the tip of a knife inserted in the centre of the loaf comes out clean. Allow to cool in the tin before turning out.

Lemon poppyseed loaf

2 unwaxed lemons
3 eggs
170 g (6 oz) caster sugar
180 g (6^1/$_2$ oz) plain flour
150 g (5 oz) unsalted butter, melted
3 teaspoons baking powder
pinch of bicarbonate of soda
1 tablespoon poppy seeds

Preheat the oven to 180°C (350°F) gas mark 4. Grease a loaf tin and lightly dust with flour.

Wash the lemons. Grate the zest of 1 lemon and squeeze the juice from both. In a large bowl, whisk together the eggs and sugar until thick and frothy. Gradually incorporate the flour and melted butter. With a spatula, fold in the baking powder, bicarbonate of soda, lemon juice and zest and poppy seeds. Fold just until well blended.

Pour the mixture into the prepared tin and bake for about 50 minutes, until the tip of a knife inserted in the centre of the loaf comes out clean. Allow to cool in the tin before turning out.

Candied fruit and nut loaf

50 g (1³⁄₄ oz) raisins
5 egg whites
140 g (5 oz) caster sugar
30 g (1 oz) unsalted butter, melted
80 g (2³⁄₄ oz) plain flour
60 g (2 oz) walnut pieces
100 g (3¹⁄₂ oz) candied fruit,
finely chopped
pinch of salt

Soak the raisins in water or rum. Preheat the oven to 180°C (350°F) gas mark 4. Grease a loaf tin and lightly dust with flour.

In a bowl, beat the egg whites until firm. Gradually beat in the sugar until stiff and glossy

With a spatula, fold in the butter, flour, walnuts, drained raisins and candied fruit. Mix gently to combine.

Pour the mixture into the prepared tin and bake for about 50 minutes, until the tip of a knife inserted in the centre of the loaf comes out clean. Allow to cool in the tin before turning out.

Apple, raisin and walnut cake

1 tablespoon raisins
3 eggs
170 g (6 oz) caster sugar
180 g (6½ oz) plain flour
150 g (5 oz) unsalted butter, melted
2 teaspoons baking powder
pinch of bicarbonate of soda
200 g (7 oz) grated apples
60 g (2 oz) walnut pieces
½ teaspoon ground cinnamon

Soak the raisins in water for 30 minutes. Preheat the oven to 180°C (350°F) gas mark 4. Grease a loaf tin and lightly dust with flour.

In a large bowl, whisk together the eggs and sugar until thick and frothy. Gradually incorporate the flour and melted butter. With a spatula, fold in the baking powder, bicarbonate of soda, drained raisins, apples, walnuts and cinnamon. Fold just until well blended.

Pour the mixture into the prepared tin and bake for about 50 minutes, until the tip of a knife inserted in the centre of the loaf comes out clean. Allow to cool in the tin before turning out.

Marble cake with almonds

2 tablespoons milk
2 tablespoons unsweetened cocoa powder
3 eggs
170 g (6 oz) icing sugar
180 g (6½ oz) plain flour
150 g (5 oz) unsalted butter, melted
3 teaspoons baking powder
75 g (2¾ oz) dark chocolate
(minimum 70% solids), grated
50 g flaked almonds

Preheat the oven to 180°C (350°F) gas mark 4. Grease a loaf tin and lightly dust with flour.

Mix together the milk and cocoa powder in a small bowl. Set aside.

In a large bowl, whisk together the eggs and sugar until thick and frothy. Add the baking powder to the flour and gradually incorporate into the eggs and sugar. Add the melted butter. Divide the mixture equally between two bowls. In the first bowl, gently fold in the milk, cocoa powder and the grated chocolate. In the second bowl, fold in the almonds.

Pour half the chocolate mixture into the prepared tin, top with half the almond mixture. Then add the remaining half of the chocolate mixture and finish with the rest of the almond mixture, Using a knife, swirl gently through all the layers just enough to marble. Bake for about 50 minutes, until the tip of a knife inserted in the centre of the loaf comes out clean. Allow to cool in the tin before turning out.

Mixed berry loaf

3 eggs
125 g (4 oz) caster sugar
100 g (3½ oz) plain flour
100 g (3½ oz) wholemeal flour
80 g (2¾ oz) unsalted butter, melted
3 teaspoons baking powder
pinch of bicarbonate of soda
1 plain yogurt
300 g (11 oz) mixed berries
(blueberries, raspberries, blackberries,
redcurrants, etc.)

Preheat the oven to 180°C (350°F) gas mark 4. Grease a loaf tin and lightly dust with flour.

In a large bowl, whisk together the eggs and sugar until thick and frothy. Gradually incorporate both the flours and melted butter. With a spatula, fold in the baking powder, bicarbonate of soda, yogurt and berries. Fold just until well blended.

Pour the mixture into the prepared tin and bake for about 50 minutes, until the tip of a knife inserted in the centre of the loaf comes out clean. Allow to cool in the tin before turning out.

glossary

bicarbonate of soda This fine white powder is an indispensable raising agent ingredient when baking sweet cakes. Just a pinch will lighten the mixture and makes it easier to digest. It is readily available in large supermarkets and sometimes in at the chemist's (be sure to indicate that it is for culinary use). Always use the quantities indicated in the recipe.

candied fruit Fruit that has been cooked in syrup, then coated with sugar. When baking with candied fruit, be sure to dust it with flour before adding to the mixture so that the pieces do not sink to the bottom.

capers in salt These are the smallest and most sought after form of capers, and are usually found in specialist delicatessens. Before using, they should be rinsed under running water and then left to drain in a colander. Alternatively, they can be soaked in cold water for 15 minutes.

dusting a cake tin To ensure that you cake won't stick to the sides and bottom of the tin, grease it well with butter, then sprinkle in some flour and tilt the tin to spread evenly. Tap the tin firmly and tip out any excess flour.

feta Greek cheese made from goat or sheep's milk, with a hard and crumbly texture. It is sold in slices, or cubed in jars with a marinade of olive oil and herbs.

mozzarella Fresh, stringy cheese, in the form of a ball, made from the curdled milk of cows or buffalo. This is readily available in most large supermarkets and Italian delicatessens.

parmesan Very hard cheese, made from cows' milk. Ageing depends on the type, but the famous Italian variety, Parmigiano-Reggiano, is aged for at least 2 years before it can be sold. It is best to buy whole chunks of Parmesan to grate as needed; the ready-grated cheese has less flavour and does not keep well as it dries out quickly.

peeled tomatoes Tomatoes that have had the skins removed before they are canned, sometimes also flavoured with basil and other herbs. These are widely available in a variety of different forms including whole, chopped or crushed as in passata.

pesto This sauce, also known as *pistou*, is made from a purée of basil, garlic, pine nuts, Parmesan, olive oil and coarse salt (see page 4).

pine nuts These are the seeds from the cone of several varieties of pine trees. Available in most large supermarkets, in the dried fruit and nut section.

pink peppercorns These are not true peppercorns but the dried berry of a South American rose plant. They are found in large supermarkets or speciality food stores, either dried or packed in vinegar. Adding these pink peppercorns to a dish gives it an attractive appearance as well as pleasant flavour.

poppyseeds These come from a plant that is cultivated especially for its seeds, used mainly in bread, cakes and pastries. Poppyseeds are available in large supermarkets and health food stores.

pumpkin cut into quarters, remove the seeds and peel. Cooks very quickly.

ricotta This cheese is made from the whey left over after making other cows' milk cheeses. The name derives from the Italian for 're-cooking'. Its texture and flavour make it a useful ingredient for both sweet and savoury dishes. Ricotta can be found in most supermarkets, usually in tubs.

sun-dried tomatoes Known as *pomodori secchi* in Italy, these are traditionally dried in the sun, then preserved in oil. To make them at home, dry out the tomatoes in a low oven for about 3 hours. Transfer to a sterilized jar and marinate with garlic, olive oil, salt and pepper for 2–3 weeks (see page 4). These are also available in most large supermarkets and Italian delicatessens.

whipping cream This cream contains at least 35% butterfat, enabling it to be whipped, unlike single cream that has 18% and cannot be whipped.

wholegrain mustard Dijon-style mustard with the addition of whole mustard seeds.

zest Very thin strips of lemon or other citrus rind, used to flavour sweet and savoury dishes, and some drinks.

crème fraîche Much used in French cooking, crème fraîche is double cream to which a fermenting agent is introduced after pasteurization, giving it a more lively taste. It is eminently suitable for savoury dishes, and is a pleasant alternative to whipped cream on fresh fruit and desserts. If preferred, thick, creamy yogurt and soured cream make good alternatives.

Shopping : Yves Deshoulières/ Blanc d'Ivoire

© Marabout 2001
text © Ilona C.
photographs © Akiko Ida

© Hachette 2001
This edition © 2003 Hachette Illustrated UK, Octopus Publishing Group, 2–4 Heron Quays, London E14 4JP
English translation by JMS Books LLP (email: moseleystrachan@blueyonder.co.uk)
Translation © Octopus Publishing Group

A CIP catalogue for this book is available from the British Library

ISBN: 1 84430 031 5

Printed by Tien Wah, Singapore